With best wishes
for a wonderful Christmas
Season -

Napi
(Naomi Barnard)

December 1, 1980

THE WONDER OF CHRISTMAS

The Wonder of Christmas

NAOMI HOLT BARNARD

BROADMAN PRESS
Nashville, Tennessee

© Copyright 1979 • Broadman Press.
All rights reserved.

4251–65
ISBN: 0–8054–5165–X

Dewey Decimal Classification: 811
Subject heading: CHRISTMAS

Library of Congress Catalog Card Number: 78–67996
Printed in the United States of America.

For my mother, my friends who believed in me, and for my children without whom this could not have been written

About the Author

Naomi Holt Barnard, called "Nopi" by most, writes that "people place high with me, especially the warm, outgoing, giving persons who fill the world with sunshine, even on dark days." Nopi herself fits into that category.

Nopi's pace as an author/mother/homemaker/journalist leaves one breathless. She publishes books, writes inspirational columns for newspapers, and is on the staff of Augusta College (in Augusta, Georgia, where the Barnards live). She also works with her husband, Doug Barnard, Jr., who is a United States congressman from their district.

The Barnards have three children, Pam (now Chafee), Lucy, and Doug III. Lucy is attracted to black cats and has two, "Boogie" and "Fluff."

Nopi serves in many community and church events. She is the "Poet Laureate of Augusta" and admits that for many years she was a "closet" poet.

Foreword

Christmas in America has become a much maligned and commercialized celebration. There is a need to learn to observe it in a fashion that would retain the spirit of the holiday and, at the same time, fit into today's life-style.

No one would like to scrap the Christmas trees, gift giving, and joy of the holiday. But we do need to temper our celebration spiritually. We need to approach all that is involved in the season in the right frame of mind. We also need to decide what is essential in our planning. We need to omit what can be dispensed with without spoiling the season.

For a number of years I have studied just what happens at Christmas in our house and in the homes of others. We Americans are an enthusiastic people. We work at everything we do valiantly, and Christmas has succumbed to this good trait with results that are not always happy.

Even for non-Christians, there is a spiritual aura about Christmas. Because of this, it is an appropriate time for Christians to display the real meaning of Christmas in overt ways, such as our attitudes toward others.

Christmas is a blessed season. It ends the year, and

it should begin a fresh new year in a spirit of Christian living. To accomplish this we must learn not to work so hard at celebrating and spend more time with our inside feelings and motives.

We must limit our buying to those items which can best show our love, and we must limit our cooking and decorating to a point just short of total fatigue. Neither children nor friends are able to love distraught people.

And we should focus our souls on why we are "getting ready." Perhaps we can find again the real "miracle of Christmas."

Nopi Barnard

CONTENTS

The Miracle of Christmas

So long ago, yet still so near each time
we hear the bells of Christmas chime.
So long ago that love came down
and still we hear the same angelic sound
when hearts expand to reach immortal size,
and hope shines out from desperate eyes
that search for love and joy and peace
within worn dreams that taunt and tease.

So long ago, God spoke in human form
and sent a part of him here to be born
to live and share our sorrows and our care;
to understand us when we have despair;
to answer why and what life's pattern draws,
to keep us humble, even through applause.

So long ago, God in his mercy spoke impartially
and paved the human trail for all posterity,
admission free. No toll he takes.
His gift, untaxed, without a string
attached to hear the angels sing
that life was bought for us eternally
when Christmas came so long ago
for you and me.

Certain men in history have changed the course of civilization. Pontius Pilate, Napoleon, Hitler, and Winston Churchill made ripples on time's river. But no volumes were written predicting their births. More interesting is the fact that while these leaders may have rocked the boat of history in their immediate streams, they are now only a part of history books.

The child that was born in Bethlehem is not just a historical figure. He is also a *now* person. His teaching of "Thou shalt love the Lord, thy God with all thy heart, . . . and thou shalt love thy neighbour as thyself" (Matt. 22: 37–39) is still the one bit of wisdom that can pull a sagging world together.

He is not "away in a manger." He is here, and the love that occurs when we feel his presence is the one power that gives us a promise of real joy and peace.

The miracle of Christmas is not that it happened, but that it is still happening today.

Mary

She journeyed through her foretold time,
    carried by beast and certainty
of where her soul must go;
    Innately in her being was a glow
of forces greater than her mind.
    She surged to follow
and leave behind security and self.
    Her being sure, her song was sung

R. Hester

to magnify and still endure
                              tenaciously
a mortal's life and death.
      Within God's plan
her body became a temple
      to give man's Savior breath.

After we deal with the Old Testament prophecies about Jesus' birth, we must look to Mary. The young Jewish girl, who was to be the mother of our Lord, must have been frightened. What quiet faith must have been given her!

A miracle of creation was beginning. But it was not the ordinary human birth process that women discover when they conceive and deliver human life. This was a milestone in history—a dividing time. In Mary's state of pregnancy, the ride to Bethlehem must have been uncomfortable, but her goal was established.

Mary was and is every woman—womanhood exalted through creation and motherhood, defined through training and upbringing. "Jesus increased in wisdom and stature, and in favour with God and man" (Luke 2:52). This is the same dream that every mother has for her son or daughter.

Since Mary, no woman need ever feel she is diminished because she is female. She can always remember Mary and reverently give thanks for the heritage of this faithful Hebrew girl. Christ could have come in a chariot with a host of angels. Instead, he came as every person enters this world. God, by touching Mary, gave womanhood status.

No pornographic magazine or movie can ever stain the purity of that woman of the first Christmas, or of women of today. And no woman need ever bow to crude ridicule of her person. Reverent respect was given woman through Mary in her status as the mother of our Lord.

Christmas Anticipation

Christmas is just a breath away,
across the week shines Christmas day—
we celebrate it, feel its warmth inside.
Give our loving gifts with pride.

Christmas is just a moment away,
most any time carols play,
and angels chorus through the land
when love and truth walk hand in hand.

Traditional, yes, we celebrate
the twenty-fifth, the assigned date,
but Christmas can shine through months and years
each time a loving thought appears.

Christmas is a tragedy and a blessing. It is a tragedy because we celebrate the season for such a short period. We cast all our goodwill on the world in a period of three weeks. The blessing of Christmas is that we take the time to celebrate it at all in this space age of learning.

Just why do we try to condense this joyful occasion into so little time? It might be perhaps that man is not capable of keeping his mind on spiritual values for very long at a time. We move through cycles within our own lives when we are good, not so good, or indifferent. Christmas might be called a cycle when more people feel better within themselves than usual.

Whether we are ready for Christmas or not, it always happens on schedule. We may not even be looking forward to it. We may be tired and wishing there were less to do. Still Christmas comes, and even people like the fictitious Scrooge find goodwill and peace stored in the basements of their beings, waiting to be brought into the light.

We must try to remember that Christmas is not just a time, but a deed. The date for Christmas may not be accurate, but a generous, kind, or merciful deed can make Christmas come most any Wednesday or Friday. This is one blessing that we have within us that cannot be bought or sold. It can only be sensed by its possessor and given away.

As God gave his Son to be born, so he also created us with the gift of being able to love and to accept love. This gift of love need not be given just at Christmas. It is valuable any day we choose to find it in our hearts and share it with another person.

Spirit of Christmas

"Spirit of Christmas?" The old man cried!
"How can I have it all empty inside?
"With all of my children moved far away,
"They'll just telephone me on Christmas day."

"Spirit of Christmas?" The young mother sighed.
"Why I can't leave my children to go shop outside . . .
"And I've no relatives here to take care of them:
"I feel I will never find my Bethlehem."

"Spirit of Christmas?" The merchant moaned.
"I just watch for shoplifters, answer the phone,
"and things to sell are slow to come in . . .
"I don't think Christmas will ever begin."

"Spirit of Christmas?" The teenager's laugh
echoed as he wandered on down danger's path—
Looking for a thrill or something to do . . .
Fifteen is too young—no jobs yet for you.

"Spirit of Christmas?" A grandmother paused
and wondered just what in her life had caused
the sinking feeling . . . her children all grown
must go far away before they can come home.

"Spirit of Christmas?" The star glowed bright,
the grandmother watched babies so the young mother
      might
go shopping. The teenager called on the man, lonely
      and old;
the merchant remembered real values, not gold—
he saw the smile of the child, heard carols of song,
and knew God's love that makes us all belong.

Just what is the spirit of Christmas? It is very hard
to define. Some people chase it throughout the month
of December and never really find it. It cannot be
bought or sold. It can only be given.

The Christmas spirit can be defined as a warm, wonderful sense of peace among men or of selflessness, as shown by the life of Christ. He gave the greatest gift, trying to impress on us how we should feel and act toward each other.

Man, of all God's creatures, has the ability to feel and express love, compassion, and thoughtfulness and to demonstrate these feelings and emotions in words and actions. Sometimes we fail to acknowledge the spirit of Christmas; we are so engrossed in ourselves. We shut the world out. Our world may be defined as a large area or just by the people immediately around us in our homes.

In defining the spirit of Christmas, our home is the best place to begin. It is here that kindness, thoughtfulness, and consideration for others really begins and radiates outward. It is here that we learn to listen for the needs of others with love and concern.

Getting Ready for Christmas

How do you get ready for Christmas?
By making lists of gifts to buy.
By scenting the house with pungent greens,
And watching the gifts pile up high.

How do you make ready for Christmas?
By having a party for your friends.
Or shopping until your feet are worn
To select the right gift to send.

How do you prepare for Christmas?
You cannot quite make it start
Until you feel its spirit, love, and truth,
And joy of soul and heart.

Right after the Thanksgiving holidays we assume a collision course with the next holiday, Christmas. The gift buying, card sending, selection and making of presents proceed at a breathtaking, hectic pace, until Christmas morning. If and when we have time to stop a moment, we are almost too exhausted to enjoy and appreciate this blessed time.

Every year the question comes, How can we avoid this? Each year we know all the answers, but we disregard them.

We know that we must discern between the necessities and the unneeded frills of the season. Does Johnny want or need that extra toy we feel we must dash out and buy? Would Susie survive without the dress we chase around to select? We know she will likely exchange it. Wouldn't they rather have a pleasant mother and father, who can pay their bills, who have time to smile at them, and make them feel special with loving warmth, than frustrated creatures, who flare up at every little thing because we are weary?

Because most of us set our own paces, we can remove the burden of overdoing at Christmas. If we will take a moment each day to think about the reason for celebrating Christmas, we will be on the way toward resolving the problem. A quiet joyful moment, which allows the joy of the season of love and goodwill to pass through us, can provide enough peace to see us through the day.

We have come to think that Christmas must be celebrated in a certain way. Tradition is good: the manger scene and a special dinner. But the decorating and cooking sometime overshadow the rapport between the family members. These habits then become enemies of the Christmas season. Most of us don't need so many decorations. And we would be better off with half as much food as we prepare and consume.

As December approaches, our main vision should be inward, not outward. We need to think carefully, instead of spinning our brains; to speak quietly, rather than nervously; to be flexible, instead of insisting on our way. And we need to look with love on all we meet.

What Is Christmas?

Christmas is a string of lights
burning brightly from the heart,
where shone the first bright star
continuing now to where we are.
Christmas is the light of love
from the soul that soars above
the earthly trials and cares
that humans find within their sphere.
Here at Christmas is the time
to let our goodness glow and shine.

What makes Christmas so special to us? First we need to look at the facts on which the holiday is based.

For two thousand years these facts have not changed, although not all people believe them.

Christmas is all of the goodness of creation massed into one wondrous act of love. It is the foundation of faith in a better life. At Christmas, if we celebrate with care, we renew that faith.

In our secularization of Christmas we have used many ways, such as Santa Claus, food, trees, candles, and giftgiving, to show our concern for those less fortunate than ourselves. Sometimes we wonder if those "less fortunate" are only in need in December. But we forget this twinge of conscience before January arrives; we return to our own worlds.

Even though Christmas lasts only a few days, it is good for us. The Yuletide season is a time when, sometimes in spite of ourselves, we are a little bit better. We are better for having examined this side of ourselves.

If we analyze the season religiously, we realize that it is more than just a time to show our better selves. It is the anniversary of a heavenly event. An event so profound that, in our celebration of it, we recall our humanity. For a brief time we experience our God-given love and compassion for others.

With all of its secular trappings we are still blessed by the celebration of Christ's birth. We can only ask forgiveness for our human frailty of commercially overdoing this special time. As mortals we need crutches for the lack of depth of our souls.

Finding Christmas

I place my plastic, inanimate ornaments
on the preassembled, artificial tree;
hang a Williamsburg wreath of inedible fruit
on the front door, graciously;
push in the plug to make the window candles glow,
and know that this is not all
there is to know about Christmas.
The figures in the manger from out of the attic
are on the chest again this year;
I join the Christmas rush and pack my shopping bag
with things! and listen to recorded angels
singing of goodwill to men,
as someone in the rush of shopping
tramples on my toes.
I tie my packages with original, wrapped designs
and bows, fill my house with the aroma
of traditional food, and wonder
as I pack it all away on the twenty-sixth,
"Was it all that good?"
In all the rush and hustle, are my feelings
real? Or will I tear them off on the day after,
like the plastic tape seal on the gifts
that I receive—leaving only pieces of bright ribbon
and a box of tired memories—and

I'm left with cold, tired turkey
and sagging cranberry sauce,
and boxes of garbage to throw out
and no time to consider the love and care
that comes from the ancient star,
that I remove from the tiny manger,
and suddenly I know with a prayer
that Christmas is always here,
No matter where!
Right where love and I are!

Those of us who have lived through a few Christmases know that this season fulfills the need of the human heart to be a little more than it is, to love a little more than it has, and to show that love in some overt way.

Christmas is thanksgiving that the souls of men and women can reach for higher aspirations. We can still befriend those friendless and hopeless ones who reach for help along the streets and alleys. We can help the sorrowing ones with tears to share, who wait to shed their cares upon the hope of Christmas.

Christmas is found in the lights that gleam and glow. It glows not from the artificial or real flame, but from the reflections of caring that we show. We find Christmas in eyes that look with love on those we meet and bless them in his holy name as we pass them on the street.

The Christmas wreath is a ring of love. The green tree is a symbol of eternal life and the candles are the eternal flame of God's care which always lights our way.

As we carol the music of Christmas, our voices are lifted in a song of rapture that in our lowly humanity, we have been given a time such as Christmas to stretch our beings toward becoming—as we find Christmas within us.

The Christmas Tree

From out its native soil, sawed and torn
along somewhere to be reborn
to celebrate a time it never knew
between the earth and lonely blue
sky it has reached for in its height . . .
Like us, a tree must search for light.

Removing the dead tree has always made me sad. Cutting a tree, standing it in a solution to keep it from being a fire hazard, and dressing it with glitter and glow for its one big binge, can seem a little wasteful. Perhaps this element of sacrifice is why living trees have become popular.

Trees have always been special for those who see beauty in nature. Whether trees have tinsel or lights or stand straight and alive, they have lessons for us that can be used in self-understanding.

Since Christmas is ultimately connected with sacrifice, the idea of the cut tree blends with the idea of selfless giving. Just as parents sacrifice at Christmas to obtain a toy a child would like, so trees sacrifice life for the celebration of a season.

While it is living the tree offers protection against storms and provides shade during the heat of the days. Likewise, Christmas reminds us of God's protective concern for us expressed so perfectly in this one gift.

As we attempt to show our love at Christmas, we are aware that love is hard to express. Perhaps this accounts for the accumulated elaborateness of our secular Christmas season.

After all, our Lord finally had to give his life to show us just how much he loved us.

December Diary

Dear Lord:

Today my body has been made weary with the "getting ready" for your birthday. There was one salesclerk who would have been cross, but I managed to cheer her with a smile and some empathy. Her feet were probably sorer than mine, but I know you understand these physical problems.

So often all of us would be kinder, but for a head aching; some would be gentle, if some physical function had not gone wrong.

Help me to ignore these problems of the human body. Forgetting them is better sometimes than placating them.

Shopping is a problem. A great blob of love forms right on top of my common sense, and sometimes it almost causes me to buy more expensive gifts than I should, as I expand lovingly with the spirit of the season. I must remember also to remind our children that Christmas is not just a shopping expedition; it is a blessed trip through love and concern.

The harmonious carols are beginning to permeate my cold, everyday heart. As I walk along, I almost float right off the pavement. I feel a little guilty at having so much joy. I am not overly blessed; maybe I am just aware of all my blessings.

Dear Lord, how can I ever fail to believe in your goodness when you cause such a glow inside me—a million candles lighted?

You will have to help me choose my gifts. Guide my selections so that I may show my heart and not my purse. I want you to be a part of the present too.

Help me to find the time to provide for those around me who are lonely, deprived, or old, and I shall be grateful to you. Goodnight, Dear Lord. Amen.[1]

Getting the Christmas Spirit

The automobiles are gathered nose to nose
around the markets of merchandise.
The checkout-counter lines are long
sometimes, as we stand and agonize
whether the gift we chose will speak
our soul-felt cheer,

here in this Yuletide season of another year.
We check our lists and plan
for parties and for "swapping" and for "giving"
and wonder how we'll make it
through the rush alive.
Our feet are tired, a tire is flat . . .
no dinner made tonight. What happened
to our Christmas? So rosy and so bright?
The checkbook balance inches down,
the new year's bills we dread.
The church play needs an angel crown,
and a Santa suit of red.
The tree's not trimmed, the wreath's not hung,
and Johnny has a cold. The other kids are jealous
and won't do as they are told.
We worry if our gifts are right,
will their childish eyes glow?
Have we guessed just what they'll like—
the bikes, the dolls—oh no!
Forgot the cookies and they burned—
well, sugar's not so high!
There goes the telephone again—
I think I'm going to cry!

But when the lights shine in their eyes . . .
and carols start to ring . . .
Somehow, it was all worth the rush,
and I hear angels sing. . . .
"Oh come all ye faithful come!"
The love spreads tranquilly . . .
and we'd work just as hard again
to feel so joyously . . .
this kindly feeling in our hearts . . .
this love song in our souls.
If Christmas makes us feel this way,

it's worth the Yuletide toll.
We each are due some joy before
we leave this beautiful earth.
We may not own a lot of things,
but this one thing we're worth.
God's love is due to each lone soul,
child and woman and man.
The lights of Christmas promise this,
and if we try we can make love shine
forth to those we know, and some who may not be
directly in our church or our vicinity.

For Christmas promises just one thing,
and this one gift to please;
Christmas gives us a precious time
when we have love and peace.

What Will You Give for Christmas?

"I'll be glad when it's over!"
I hear people say
as they spoil the spirit of Christmas day.
All this tinsel spending on cash register row,
and many more places than time to go.

It makes me sad to hear them despair
when the carols of Christmas lilt through the air—
When men's hearts should grow to match the love
that encircles the earth from the star above.

"I'm glad it comes but once a year," I hear
as I wave good-bye to our tree with a tear
for the laughter lost in children's eyes
and the breaking of renewed family ties.

I am grieved to see it all pass away
and settle down to the workaday
world where it's not in style
to remember the teachings of the Christmas child—
Of his love that frees us from fears within,
Of his peace and care on which we still can depend.

We might be able to avoid the attitude of wishing Christmas would go away if we were a little more careful about what we give for Christmas.

Christ's teaching of "Man shall not live by bread alone" (Matt: 4:4) could be spread over the Christmas season with good results. If we mortals could learn that we can give our love to others without wrapping it in colorful paper, we could celebrate Christmas cheerfully.

Christmas Eve Diary

Dear Lord,

It is the eve of your birthday. I wonder if you look down in amazement and excitement at all the human customs now performed in your honor.

Do you count the Christmas lights as birthday candles? When we forget to include you in our plans, does your heart ache?

Are you astounded at all of the lovely, glittering mountains of material objects that we heap upon each other? Do you wonder why we forget that, although giving a gift is a good way to show love, sometimes just being remembered is our very best gift? Do you smell the baking, and the roasting and hope that none of your children are hungry tonight?

Dear Lord, I've made all kinds of lists to try to remember everyone I should. I've checked the lists and tried, though I am a little tired at this hour, to keep smiling at my family. I want them to remember this Christmas as a happy time with me. Sometimes, with ten things to do and little time in which to do them, it is hard to stay pleasant. But, if I concentrate, I can hear your voice saying, "Be ye kind one to another" (Eph. 4:32). And it helps—it really does. Thank you!

I try to remember this need for kindness even when those tired clerks are cross. They are obviously wishing for the closing hour when they may join their own families. I must also forgive that person who, in his haste, tries to push me from his path.

Give me patience, Lord, to keep your special day in a peaceful, loving way. May your love radiate through me to my family. Help them to remember that there is giving for them, as well as receiving, as we unwrap our gifts of love for each other.

I am tired tonight, and I know I shall be tired tomorrow. Please rest my mind and body through the night, so that I may allow you to join with us in the celebration of your joyous occasion.

Happy birthday, Lord. Goodnight. Amen.[2]

Keeping Christmas

The Christmas streets are still tonight,
the baby has been born within the lighted
window of the store,
and no one stands to watch it anymore
within the creche; its statues
kneeling around
beneath a false, bright star . . .
no audience is found
for musical messages of love and cheer:
Christmas has come and gone for another year.

What do we do with the remains of Christmas? The decorations go into the attic. Gifts are swapped or used or stored away to give to someone else. The home is cleared for business as usual, and the business is steamed up for profit as usual. Friendly greetings float forever somewhere on the waves of time; maybe they end up in a galaxy of space where they will be no more understood than they were sometimes here on earth.

The bills come in for the things we probably couldn't afford, which we bought in cheerful abandon. The profiteering practices continue from Wall Street to

Main Street, from labor to staff to management, or wherever people are climbing ladders toward some tangible goal—as if Christmas never happened.

Christmas came and was dealt with this year, and we can write it in our diaries. Now it's back to "do unto others before they do unto you," get your message in first, and don't give your opposition a chance.

It may sound like bitter medicine, but we have almost learned to celebrate Christmas perfectly. We do it with flair, abandon, originality in our gift wraps, Christmas trees, parties—even our church affairs. For these few days, we paste smiles on our faces and vocalize in mellow tones of good cheer. Then whammo! It's all over; if you can't cut it, get out of the game!

We do celebrate well, but we are guilty much of the time of not keeping Christmas well. It's too bad that we can't open savings accounts at Christmas and deposit some of the surplus smiles, good cheer, fun, and comradeship to be used during the rest of the year.

Christmas did not start as a celebration of a few weeks. Its interest is annual. Its benefits are compounded. If we learn to use them, they will accrue more than the best securities.

You need not be a member of a certain church to keep Christmas. You must be a member of the human race and God's large family. The door to Christmas love is marked "concern for others." If we learn to live without ever entering that door, we cannot keep Christmas in December or any other part of the year.

This year is a good time to begin practicing the "keeping of Christmas" again. Those of us who have tried it have learned that even the failures that come over the stormy days of the new year can be smoother.

Leaving Christmas behind in December is cheating ourselves of one of the blessings that will never appear on a monthly charge account.

Christmas is our free, end-of-the-year, eternal blessing.

Silence Is a Secret Weapon

Silence is a gift available to everyone. Many people may not have the ability to speak or to give great orations; some may not be able to communicate well, but everyone has the ability to hold his tongue.

The Ecclesiastes Scripture, "There is a time to every purpose" (3:1), includes the "time to keep silence" (3:4). There is also a time to speak, and knowing the difference can prevent a lot of problems for us.

One year, just after Christmas, I seemed to be screaming incessantly at our three children, who were at their most mischievous ages. Suddenly I lost my voice. I was amazed at how quiet the whole household became. The children began to whisper back at me, instead of screeching. The peace and quiet was very comforting to my frazzled nerves, which had been pulled apart by all the Christmas responsibilities.

My throat ached when I spoke, and I necessarily weighed each word I said: Is it absolutely necessary to respond vocally? I learned a great lesson.

Now, I find that when someone speaks unkindly to

me—either in person or by telephone—if I refuse to respond and remain silent for a few seconds, I can go on to another subject, avoid arguments, and maintain my self-control. When I do speak when I should have remained silent, all kinds of problems emerge: people become angry; I lose my composure, and the day goes awry.

If someone says something that seems to require a comment, I try to remember that what I say can be misconstrued or misunderstood; it can be misquoted; or it can involve me in a situation that I would have preferred to evade.

Losing my voice was one of the best gifts I have ever received at Christmas time.

Time for a Religious Commercial

We pause for a commercial, Lord,
   somewhere between the line
of dark and dawn of Thy
divinely revealed will.
The chatter wanders on—
nor is it still
for meditation—thoughts
to lift the soul,
a clatter-shatter sound by
knob control.
Please lead us on your way,

soft-sell or cross
we carry—help us bear
the pitch and toss
your message holds
between life's programmed way;
A verbal advertisement not to stray.
Just interrupt us Lord,
Our journey needs a rest—
Intrigue and sooth our souls
with what is best.[3]

There are times at Christmas when we feel that commercialism is a great monster. It seems to be devouring the spirit of the season so precious to us. We hear the beautiful carols by radio, interspersed with glib sales pitches; sometimes it seems the angels are actually doing the selling.

A few moments of quiet alone can clear our ears and prepare them to hear the real message of Christmas. Maybe commercials are necessary in our modern culture. Christ said, "Render therefore unto Caesar the things which are Caesar's; and unto God the things that are God's" (Matt. 22:21). The balance is delicate, but we can achieve it if we don't lean too hard on the dollar side.

We must take time for a few religious commercials during the day. We must stop and remember why we are here and what we are celebrating. The secular commercials will fall into their places. If we give God equal time, our souls will rise to the level of love and gratitude that will bring us the peace we seek.

Why Ask for More?

Why should we really ask for more?
We have four walls, a roof, a floor,
a stove for cooking, some books for reading,
a dear old dog whose eyes are pleading
to share a place beside our chair—
just being there.

Why should we really ask for more?
We have some food, a friendly door,
some children here to rear and love,
a grassy lawn, the sky above,
just living, loving, singing, giving
through smile and tear.

Why should we really ask for more?
No one has needed it before.
Why covet what we do not need,
Why climb and struggle till we bleed
When essential only is human love
and God above?

We are a success-oriented nation. Everything must
be a little larger, better, newer, fresher, more beautiful, or stronger than what we have had before. When
this idea is applied in moderation, it may not be wrong.

The drive for success has brought progress to our country. It has carried us through some bad times.

Our zealous search for success sometimes overshadows our current blessings. This is especially true at Christmas. We tend to forget that we have safe, warm homes, enough food, and fairly good health. We forget to look on our lives with appreciation as we extend ourselves toward getting something a little better or bigger for ourselves or as a gift for someone else.

Counting our blessings should have top priority at Christmas, and uppermost must be the spirit of love that we were given at the first Christmas.

Christmas Is Thanksgiving

When clouds hang low over the winter terrain
I think, "Be thankful for the rain"
that brightens colors against skies of gray.
How tragic if it all went away
or if I had no eyes to see
the hues that glimmer vividly.
As each raindrop stirs a leaf,
I hear its patter. I'm a thief
of all this gentle sound. My ears
are blessed by nature's winter tears.
And what if I were forced to stay
in just one place to work or play.
If paralyzed or my sight was gone,
I'd not be justified to groan,

not if these fingers still could pen
a line that holds my heart within
to say, "I'm thankful to thee
"for all I have . . . to live as me."

As we wait for Christmas, the weather often becomes very inclement. Rain keeps the children inside. It's difficult to entertain them. The humidity in the air keeps the fudge from setting and makes other candy sticky. People track rain and mud on the floors we have just waxed. Snow would be better if we can't have sun.

But rain is one of God's blessings. There are parts of our country without enough water. We cannot wonder why it falls on us. We can only be grateful that we are in such a time and place.

It is appropriate that Christmas is preceded by Thanksgiving. It should put us in a better frame of mind to receive the Christ child, who came to bless us and teach us how to live.

This is the first thanksgiving item on our Christmas list.

Christmas Is for Seeing

Bartimaeus called upon the Christ;
He did not cite his sin—
so scolded was he that he dared to shout

above the human din
that followed out of Jericho;
a beggar was not fit to noise forth so.

"Have mercy"—he still did not say the wrong
that plagued him. Sacrifice and song
of chants had failed to ever heal
the ill that made him beggar.
His appeal was heard by Christ,
who knew that he'd no sight,
yet bade him name his very need for light:
"Lord, give me here my sight!"
He spoke our basic sin,
a lack of vision from without, within.

As Bartimaeus, I would pray for sight
when eyes still see, but
darkness is a blight
across my soul. Restore my faith and cast
away my street-stained robe, sunglass mask.
Contrite before thee now I kneel
and go thy way, not mine: Yours to reveal.

One characteristic that most of us share is that we
can look at something and still not see it. We look
our children over in the morning to see that they are
clean and neatly dressed, but we sometimes fail to
see what our children really need most.

We look at our spouses as we say, good morning
or welcome home, and we don't see them as they really
are.

December is a time for giving. But in order to give
we must see. This kind of seeing is not just looking
at the pretty decorations or glittering gifts offered for
sale. It's a time for seeing with the heart, for reading

the human need to be loved, to belong somewhere, to be accepted by someone, and to be looked upon as an individual.

Loneliness is a human plague, incurable with drugs. We must have vision to see the loneliness where it exists. There is need waiting behind frightened eyes; we need the ability to see, with eyes of love, through whatever shell may have been built to enclose it.

Five Minutes More

Christmas is a time for rushing around, sometimes almost blindly, trying to get everything done. We make long lists of chores, of foods to be prepared, of gifts to buy, and of places to go.

One minute can mean a lot in our scheme of activities at Christmas, and five minutes sometimes is an eternity. We can be more gracious and more fruitful if we remember to include our Lord as we speed along through the day.

I do not ask for grace to steer
beyond tomorrow's door;
I only ask thy guiding hand
for just five minutes more.

Tomorrow's problems may be vast,
we know not what's in store;
but now I only ask from thee
for just five minutes more!

Five minutes more of strength and grace
to help me hold my tongue;
five minutes more to hold my place,
climb up another rung
along the ladder that looms high
when stared at from afar.

I do not ask that I may fly
or chase a flitting star;
I only ask for patience
that is the center of life's core;
All I ask from you, dear Lord,
Is just five minutes more.

Christmas Greetings

Whenever I receive a Christmas card,
I breathe a silent prayer
for the one who thoughtfully sent it
to ask God's loving care.

Blessings are asked on every house
that was the origin,
prayers lifted that these homes might know
peace and goodwill toward men.

Some cards are glittering,
silver and gold;
some small with less to say;
but every time one comes to me,
I hear Christmas carols play.

We are told each December just when to mail our Christmas cards, and the inflationary prices on stamps has certainly curtailed the quantity of cards once received. Most people now limit their Christmas cards to those persons and relatives who will not be seen and wished a merry Christmas in person.

Mailing such cards is a joy equaled only by receiving them. It is such a thrill to get a card from a dear, old friend or relative with a handwritten note. Much time is spent adding these personal notes to our own cards. With the number of cards sent and received becoming smaller, we have more time to actually enjoy each one and think kindly and prayerfully as we open its merry Christmas greeting.

Midnight Vow

I was much too busy to hear one small boy
as he showed me the picture of a coveted toy.
Hurrying about, I said, "Wait a while. . . ."
"I'll hear about it when I finish ironing this pile."
Now he's asleep, at peace in his bed,
Face all clean and prayers all said.
I suddenly recall I did not find the time
to listen to the wish of this child of mine.
I vow tomorrow, if that day comes to me,
I'll listen intently, quite patiently
to a tow-headed boy who gets taller each day,

who shows every sign he'll be growing away.
I wonder if I, when someday he is gone,
will wonder how I preferred the telephone
and will wish again for an eight-year-old boy
to want to show Mother his most coveted toy.

Fritz Perls, the originator of the Gestalt psychology, said we do unto others as we do unto ourselves. His theory is those who do not listen to and accept themselves probably were not listened to and accepted as children. Those who are critical of others are probably very critical of themselves.

In order to help our children accept themselves, we must learn to focus our attention on them. Half an ear is no ear at all. At Christmas, in all the rush, it is difficult to force ourselves to listen. We look back sadly on the times when we could have been listening to our children and passed them up for busyness.

Christmas is for caring and listening.

Gifts That Are Free

You cannot buy your sense of smell
or the sight with which you see;
You cannot buy the sound
of a musing honeybee
or purchase all the music
from birds that freely sing;

the viewing of a sunset—
these come to knave or king.
Your money may buy plastic, metal,
steel, or chrome,
but it will not ever quite purchase
a loving, happy home.
You cannot buy good health or peace
or bargain for a friend;
he may become your enemy
when your cash he cannot spend.
The gifts of life are there to hear,
the beauty for those who'll see;
no money is needed to buy them:
like love, they're yours for free.

As the Yuletide season approaches and we begin to make out our gift lists, there are some presents which are not for sale.

Christmas will be more meaningful if we remember the blessing of our senses. When we find an item that is too expensive for us to buy, we can thank God for our eyesight to see it. We can also be aware of how much more beautiful the natural world is.

The Most Difficult Love

To love my enemy
is a superhuman task,
but this he told me I must do.

He did not ask
if I would try,
as he was upon the cross;
He did not modify.
He simply forgave and loved the men
who sealed his fate.
And I—I can do nothing less
than love my foe
at his command . . .
or try.

Christmas is a good time to practice love. Through the year we build up enmities and unhappy feelings. Sometimes this happens against our wishes, but nevertheless the feelings are very real.

To remember to think lovingly of those persons who may not have been fair to us is difficult; but once we do, the hurt will dissolve, as water does by sunlight. We'll feel better "all over," as a child would say.

One does not have to be "goody-goody" to practice the art of loving. Love is a form of therapy. We are not so much doing the estranged person a favor as we are healing ourselves. Love can almost be considered selfish if it is selfless because it is good medicine for our beings.

It is not always necessary to overtly confront our adversary with our feelings of love. When you love someone it shows in some way, and the person loved will usually respond.

Love is magic. It is a presence that makes the sun shine on a gloomy day. It is the smile that chases the tears away.

If your adversary is unable to respond to your psychic feeling of love, do not be perturbed. Continue your feelings because if you are able to cleanse yourself of enmity against someone, you have won half a battle. And you can be happy with that victory.

. . . And Then They Send You Roses

You wonder if you've done
everything quite right;
you wake and say a prayer
in the middle of the night
for the child who is away
at camp or off at school;
will everyone who meets them
remember the golden rule?
Or did you say, "I love you"
before they left to go—
. . . and then they send you roses.

You've hassled them to church
with straggled hair and awry dress;
you've spoken shortly to them
so much, you must confess
you've often failed to listen
when some tale they tried to tell.
You've even frowned unconsciously
as you worked away, as well—
. . . and then they send you roses.

If hindsight could be perfection
a perfect parent you would be,

but you're just another blot
of mortal humanity—
you only hope and trust
until your eyelids finally close
they'll still remember you
and maybe send you just one rose.

Parenthood is the most difficult of all occupations. It is also the most rewarding when children remember you, even though you feel undeserving.

Only we parents know our shortcomings, and they are numerous. We do not like to discuss them because we begin to judge ourselves. We are not qualified to do that. Only God is qualified to judge.

Sometimes, in the midnight hours when we think of all the things we might have done or said, the clouds of misery come down close to our hearts. We wonder if we could have done better. The next day one of these little people we have thrust into the world remembers us in some way. We are showered with roses. Their blessed perfume follows us into the dark nights of the years to come when we forget to be grateful for our blessings and begin to remember our deficiencies. It's then that we must smell the scent of roses given long ago.

"Lazarus, Come Forth"

"Lazarus, come forth,"
He cries to me
here in my web
of humanity . . .
the darkness fades
and prisms shine,
as I walk forth
in his design.

One of the most moving scenes in the recent film *Jesus of Nazareth* was the raising of Lazarus from the dead. The scene was superb. As I watched the movie, a thought came to mind. So many times we, too, are in a corpse-like state, removed from God's blessing. We are not responding to his call to come out of our man-made shells and live in his light.

The habits, attitudes, demands, and chores of the world bind us as the dismal, sepulchral cloths wrap the lifeless mummies in the tombs. By responding to his call, we can cast off the human weights that prevent us from living in the sunshine of his spirit.

Christ did not intend for us to be morbid souls. His first miracle was changing water into wine at a wedding feast. He carried our burdens for us that we might be joyful because of his presence in our lives. "Come unto me all ye that . . . are heavy laden, and I will give you rest" (Matt. 11:28). The message is still clear two thousand years later. We do not have to live in darkness and despair. Joy and peace are ours when we respond to his summons, and "Come forth" (John 11:43).

A Christmas Resolution

This year, I promise myself I shall not get bone-weary working at the celebration of Christmas. I shall not cook until the sight of food nauseates me, my family reminds me of a bunch of vultures waiting to pounce, and I behave like a worn-out witch.

If the only way to find time to sit down with my children and enjoy them is to feed them sandwiches, that's what I'll do. I shall buy enriched bread, the best peanut butter, and ham, cheese. My baking will be done a month in advance. I'll serve my simple meals with a smile, instead of a tired frowning. And I shall try to get my children to help with the preparations even though I can manage twice as quickly alone.

I shall try to remember that a happy face is worth more than all the gourmet meals. If I succeed in keeping my priorities in order, I will have done my best toward making a happy Christmas my children will not forget.

I am not making these resolutions in haste. They are the product of years of fatigue from holiday preparations and depression. There have been many times I have not felt the joy that Christmas deserves. Sometimes I think we women mistake martyrhood for motherhood and housework for happiness.

Recently, as I bought a Christmas gift, the young salesclerk said, "Isn't Christmas awful?" (I think she meant "dreadful.")

"No," I replied. "It's people's attitudes about Christmas that are awful."

Her look of puzzlement was justified. We have tended to change Christmas from a season of peace and serenity to a time of turmoil and trial. Our attitudes imply that if everything isn't done perfectly, December twenty-fifth won't come.

Here is the good news: Christmas comes and goes no matter how much or how little we do. If we look back over our lives and select the Christmas which was the happiest, it will not be the one where we did everything perfectly.

Christmas Reading

How long since you've read your children a story,
sitting beside you, eyes young and bright?
Have you recently read them just one tiny Scripture
with your voice soft and low in the night?

Cuddled beside you, they're safe in their kingdom;
the sofa or chair in worn state is your throne,
as you sweep sparkling language to rest in their mem'ry
of faraway places away from their home.
Pictures are formed in the action of reading;
Imagination reflects from shepherds and kings.

Tonight we read the dear Christmas story,
the children beside me, eyes young and bright;
tonight we read of the angels' bright glory,
of their carols of joy on that hallowed night.
Quiet beside me, they heard of the stable,
(my voice, I'm afraid, had a catch in its tone)
as the exalted language rested within them,
Of the small Baby Jesus, who had no home.

Tonight we read the old Christmas story,
of the Wise Men who brought gifts from afar,
And when I looked up from the book I was reading,
I saw in their eyes the light of the star.

A recent survey has shown that 8:00 to 8:30 P.M. there are 14.7 million children watching television. From 8:30 to 9:00 P.M. the number drops to 14.1 million, but from 11:00 to 11:30 P.M. there are still 2.9 million youngsters glued to the tube.

Television came upon us and we did not know what it was. At first it was a convenience. We used it as a baby-sitter to keep children amused while we did our chores. There are some programs which are acceptable and television can serve a good purpose, but it cannot replace parenting. It cannot erase the need for parents to spend time with their children. It cannot take the place of parents reading to their children. A child needs to make his own imaginary pictures and not just to depend on television's technicolor productions.

Studies show there is a definite relationship between street violence and television violence. Dr. Robert Liebert, a psychologist at the State University of New York, states, "It was not the boy's home life, not his school performance, not his family background, but the amount of television violence he viewed at age nine, which was the single most important determinant of how aggressive he was ten years later, at the age nineteen."

A recent study by the University of Utah researchers reported on children who watched an excessive amount of television. The researchers concluded that the children's normal reactions to violence become numbed. This numbing of feelings may cause an increase in violence in our society. Concern for the victims of such violence decreases.

The answer to problems of violence is the practice of the tenets of Christianity. But how can one hour of Sunday School and one hour of worship on the Lord's Day reverse the effects of forty to fifty hours of television viewing during the week?

There is only one way to destroy the effects of the television Goliath we are facing, and that is through the rock of Christian teaching.

Christmas is a good time to begin.

The Forerunner of Easter

What part of me is crucified with Thee?
Some petty sins I hide in piety—
Or is my wrong quite equal with that kiss;
Have I here, too, betrayed Your Holiness?
So cleansed I came, through Your last sacrifice.
No need to feel the pain—You paid the price
To conquer wrong with love. Such power
You handed me through faith in Calvary's hour.
I kneel convicted, but your victory
Today begins my life anew and free.[4]

The greatest miracle of Christmas is that it brings us Easter. We renew ourselves in the knowledge that Christ came for a purpose. He lived as a man, with man's temptations and problems. He felt all of our emotions, and through his grace we are freed to rise above our earthly cares.

Christ supports us not only at Christmas and Easter but also throughout all the days of our lives. We only have to ask. We need only to reach. His hand is always out beckoning us toward love and forgiveness.

The risen Christ is the spirit of Christmas.

Aftermath

The deadened tree is down
and lying on a pile of grubby garbage.
The decorating style
of ribbon, tinsel, lights,
has passed along into a closet.
The passing throng races to a destiny
of sell and buy, of fail and weep
and rise again and try.

Business as usual on leftover cheer
becomes a flat, pale duty in low gear.
Depression needles our hearts
like a deadened pine. We look
for joy but see no outward sign.
If we could find a way to preserve
this Christmas love and cheer,
we'd have a happier time
during the coming year.

It is a fact that depression after Christmas is almost certain. We have Americanized the season and put it on a pedestal as the medium through which all wrongs are righted. We wander blissfully looking for

the pail of joy at the foot of the Christmas lighted rainbow.

We have almost convinced ourselves that this should be the end aim of Christmas. But this is not true, and we soon realize that the alarm clock will shatter our morning slumber. Each day we rise and stumble with tired souls and half-awake hearts into weeks and months of problems and cares.

How can we avoid the listless where-do-I-go-from-here feeling that we wrap around ourselves after the holidays? Our eyes burn from too much television football; our digestive tracts rumble from too much rich food and drink. Loss of sleep dulling our brains, we watch the bathroom scales scornfully slap the needle much farther over than we want to see. Christmas has to be more than this. We wonder about it as we creep morbidly into our selfish shells after we have completed our Christmas celebrating.

Our attitude toward other people will help to determine whether we wear a smile or a frown. If we are thoughtless, unconcerned, and care little about what happens to anyone but ourselves, the new year will be dull for us. If we quickly forget the charitable, generous feelings we found in our hearts during Christmas, we are certain to fall into the "slough of despond." Living just within and for ourselves is a perfect way to be unhappy.

One sure way to forget about our after-Christmas depression is to think of someone else. Which child in the family requires some avid support? Whose elderly mother would welcome a brief visit from us? Is there a nursing home nearby where people are also feeling sad?

A good way to let the Christmas spirit shine into

the new year is to continue to be loving, kind, considerate, and full of good cheer. We need to remember that Christ walks with us as we move through our days, and it is his support gained through prayer that generates our courage to continue to look up.

When You Have Your Faith

When you have your faith
you have just about everything.
You know the sun will shine again,
that life will go on
even when now and then
you don't reap what you've sown
in your life. You know
that true friends will stay
beside you; that love will glow
from faces into which you have smiled
your own affection,
and that each day
must be lived within your time's frame
as if it were your last.
You do not weigh
your gifts bestowed along your path
against that of any other man. You
give as you have and as is given, receive—
rejoicing when you can sing—
because when you have your faith,
you have just about everything.

This is a parody on a well-known television commercial which has health as its main theme. Health is very important, but we are not promised strong bodies. This is a matter of genetics, environment, and how we care for ourselves. Sometimes the damage is done before we are old enough to repair it. Sometimes ill health visits us for no apparent reason.

We can meet such circumstances in the same way we face everyday procedures. When we see a traffic light turn green, we have faith that the other drivers with the red light will stop. When we fly in a plane we have faith that the pilot knows what he is doing. There are hundreds of moments in a day when we have faith in something. The important part of our philosophy is to have faith in something that is worthy of our faith. People and things may not always be worthy. They are fallible. They have faults. People can rationalize themselves right out of faith with you. Material objects break or have parts or fuels which are sometimes not available.

Governments collapse. Political figures who seemed to be honest turn out to be otherwise. Even your relatives have seemed to be less than helpful to you at times. Children go astray. Parents reprimand you when you don't feel you deserve it.

What is important? We must have faith in God. The God who came in human form to live as we do gives us a sense of security when everything else falls apart. He is the feeling of quiet power that comes to us during and after prayer. We have the consolation of calling on God when sorrow has carried us beyond the bounds of self-sustainment.

This is the same faith that has been sung, written about, and believed in for centuries. Somehow, in spite of medical advances, scientific breakthroughs, and all the human relations material which has been fed to us for the past fifty years, we still can find this faith very real when these modern tangibles fall apart and fail.

Life goes on and when we have our faith we have just about everything.

Notes

1. Naomi Barnard, "December Diary," *Christian Index,* 17 December 1971.
2. ———, "Christmas Eve Diary," *Christian Index,* 23 December 1971.
3. ———, "Time for a Religious Commercial," was originally published as "Station Break," *A Wonderful Day* (Forest Park, Ga.: Debra Lynn Company, 1974), p. 7. Used by permission.
4. ———, "The Forerunner of Easter" was originally published as "Easter Meditation," *A Wonderful Day,* p. 16. Used by permission.